Easy Activities for Every Kid

130 Activities for School and Home

by

Joan Singleton Prestine

and

Debbie Prestine Kachidurian

Fearon Teacher Aids
A Division of Frank Schaffer Publications, Inc.

Dedicated to Kelly, Megan, and Madison

Editors: Lisa Schwimmer Marier, Hanna Otero
Cover Design: Riley Wilkinson
Cover Illustration: Pat Wong
Book Design: Good Neighbor Press, Inc.

© **Fearon Teacher Aids**
A Division of Frank Schaffer Publications, Inc.
23740 Hawthorne Boulevard
Torrance, CA 90505-5927

Fearon Teacher Aids product were formerly manufactured and distributed by American Teaching Aids, Inc., a subsidiary of Silver Burdett Ginn, and are now manufactured and distributed by Frank Schaffer Publications, Inc. FEARON, FEARON TEACHER AIDS, and the FEARON balloon logo are marks used under license from Simon & Schuster, Inc.

FE11053

Table of Contents

Introduction

Teachers, parents, and caregivers are often pressed for time, so *Easy Activities for Every Kid*, a wonderful new book filled with a wealth of simple, easy-to-do activities, was created just for you. The fun activities from this book provide an increase in gross and fine motor skills, verbal and language skills, math and reading concepts, and individual and group social skills—all of which are necessary to ensure a productive and successful school experience for children.

No experience, no credentials, and no artistic ability are necessary to organize and complete any of the activities in this book. And the activities use common, inexpensive household items that are easy to clean up.

There are five main components to *Easy Activities for Every Kid*. Each component provides ideas and activities to help make your teaching time educational, enjoyable, and stress-free!

Before You Begin provides you with hints for success, ideas for materials, and information on safety, as well as activity setup and cleanup.

Creativity brings you fun, interesting activities that include collages, crafts, greeting cards, painting, and more, keeping children engrossed in their own creative tasks for hours.

Performance offers children a chance to participate in all aspects of dramatic performance—set design, making costumes and masks, make-up, and performance. In addition, children will create puppets and participate in storytelling.

Movement allows for creative physical exercise, not only improving gross motor movement and coordination, but providing fun, exciting play for children. This component provides activities in exercise, dance, games, and indoor and outdoor play.

Responsibility uses cooking and gardening activities to help children learn to be responsible for simple, interesting tasks as they create recipes and tend to their own garden.

Skills adds to the other skills learned in the preceding components, providing activities specially designed for learning skills in math, science, tactile learning, as well as how they use their senses, story-extending, and music and dance.

Feel free to use the activities and materials in any way that is appropriate for you and the children. Most of all, have fun!

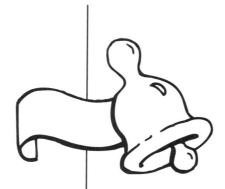

Before You Begin

Preparation can help tremendously in having a successful, fun-filled day. Following are some ideas for making the activities as fun and easy as possible.

Set Up

To give children a sense of responsibility and ownership of their projects, have them listen as you read the materials list for each activity before you begin. Then they can locate the materials and put them in just the right spot. The more children help you, the more it lightens your load.

To protect children's clothing during messy projects, keep large, old shirts handy to use as smocks.

To protect carpet, use newspaper or painter's drop cloths. Try to do messy projects on hard floors or, better yet, outside. Keep a broom and dustpan handy for quick cleanup.

To protect tables, cover them with newspaper, butcher paper, or large sheets of vinyl. Keep a sponge or paper towels nearby so the children can wipe up spills immediately.

If an activity is going to take longer than one sitting to complete, choose an area where you can safely leave materials out to avoid setting up again.

Materials

Each activity lists materials you most likely have on hand. If not, they are easily found and reasonably priced. You might want to check if you have some of the more commonly used items in stock—crayons, markers, chalk, tempera paint, paintbrushes, plain and construction paper, cardstock, cardboard, rounded scissors, and non-toxic glue.

Try to use as many recycled materials as possible. Explain to children that recycling saves our environment, saves money, and saves time shopping.

If you don't have specific materials on hand, be creative—feel free to substitute something that you think might work even better. Children are often a great source for ideas; ask them what they would use.

Many activities call for paper as a base to begin a project. Construction paper is readily available, reasonably priced, but may fade over time. Cardstock can be found in office supply and art stores and, though more expensive, is sturdy, comes in larger sizes, is available in bright colors, and doesn't seem to fade. Cardboard is available at office supply stores and may also be recycled from cardboard boxes. Butcher paper can be found in teacher and food supply stores.

Markers, pens, crayons, tempera paints, and chalk can be interchanged for several activities. Choose the instruments that appeal to you for each project.

Some activities involve food. If you feel that these activities are inappropriate for the children in your group, feel free to eliminate them.

Before beginning any activity that includes food, be certain there are no food allergies. If some children have allergies, find suitable ingredient substitutes so that every child may participate.

Keep scraps of cloth, paper, tissue, and other materials in a large plastic container. Collect bits and pieces of materials throughout the year. When you have an idea for collages or other art projects, you can bring out these left-overs for children to add to their creations.

Safety

The projects in *Easy Activities for Every Kid* are for children between the ages of three and eight. Though these projects are easy and safe to create, it is important that at least one or two adults are close by to ensure proper use of the materials.

Most of the materials used in these activities are safe for use by children. Check your glue, markers, scissors, and other materials to ensure they are appropriate for the children in your group. Make sure very young children use plastic, rounded scissors and plastic knives for cutting. Stay in close contact as children do these activities to guarantee proper usage. Follow product directions and warnings.

Before serving food as a snack, meal, or activity, be sure to check for food allergies. Some food allergies can be life-threatening.

Cleanup

To ensure a successful project, everyone needs to help clean up. If children know from the outset that cleanup is part of the activity, then it becomes a habit.

Children usually want to help clear, wash and dry dishes, and sweep the floor. Invite them to have a go at it, but keep your eye on them.

Have the children clean up outside activities with a broom or a hose.

You can make a game out of cleanup by setting a timer and seeing if children can pick up all the materials and toys before the timer rings.

Label shelves and boxes where materials belong and turn cleanup into a matching game. Children learn quickly to match items with their appropriate storing places.

Sing favorite songs while you and the children clean up. Singing passes the time more quickly and can be a happy way to complete an activity.

Hints for Successful Activities

Flexibility is critical in meeting everyone's needs and interests. If you plan a quiet activity and children are restless, set the activity aside and introduce active play. When children seem ready to focus, reintroduce the planned quiet activity.

It's best to stop an activity as you notice interest waning. If you wait too long, you may have to deal with temperaments as well as having to organize a new activity.

Weather permitting, try to have at least one activity outside each day. It's to everyone's advantage to do as many of the suggested activities outside as possible. Cleanup is easier with a broom or hose, and children enjoy the freedom of outside play.

Shared responsibility makes activities rewarding for you and the children. Have children do as much for themselves as possible—get out materials, work independently on their projects, create new ideas, lead group activities, and clean up afterwards.

During activities, it is important to remain within earshot, but try to avoid constant interaction. Distance gives children the opportunity to develop social skills, stretch their imaginations, expand their capabilities, experiment with their creativity, resolve their struggles, and become independent.

Some children are more interested in the process of an activity rather than the outcome. For a few, the end result of an activity may not be a finished project. While the children create their projects, provide them with the freedom to explore and stretch their imaginations using their own unique flair.

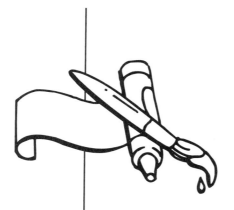

Creativity

Creativity and ideas come in many forms. The activities on the next pages give children exciting opportunities to explore their own special creativity!

Collages

It doesn't take a lot to stimulate most children's creativity. They are apt to jump into collage projects with little concern for the outcome and be pleasantly surprised with the results. With miscellaneous items, paper, cardboard, and white glue or paste, children can spend hours creating. For many, the fun is in turning discarded materials into keepsakes to hang on walls, display on tables, or give as gifts.

Cut and Paste

Children will spend hours cutting and pasting almost anything. Provide products for children to cut up. Set up a work area by a wastebasket, or invite children to sit in a large box to make cleaning up later a cinch! Have them use rounded scissors to cut shapes out of paper or cut pictures from old magazines, recycled catalogs, or wrapping paper. Some children may want a theme for their collages, while others may not. When they finish, have children glue or paste their cutouts onto construction paper to create original designs.

You will need

construction paper
glue or paste
old magazines, recycled
catalogs, wrapping paper
rounded scissors
wastebasket or large box

Collages

You will need

cardstock or plywood
glue
gravel (purchased at garden shops)
markers
recycled tuna cans
slotted spoon
tempera paint
waxed paper

Gravel Mosaics

For this activity, children can transform the materials before they use them artistically! First, the gravel must be dyed. Children enjoy watching the gray gravel transform into brightly colored gravel! Then children can use the colorful gravel to turn simple drawings into three-dimensional pictures. To begin the dye process, help children place gravel into shallow tin cans filled with small amounts of liquid tempera paint. Each child can decide when, in the soaking process, his or her gravel is the desired color. After each child has decided on the proper color, he or she can carefully scoop the gravel onto waxed paper with a slotted spoon. While the gravel dries, children can draw pictures on pieces of plywood or cardstock. Once the gravel is dry, children can glue colored gravel onto their pictures to make Gravel Mosaics.

You will need

construction paper
glue or paste
items that begin with the letter of the week—for example the letter C could include cotton balls, candles, crayons, cans, and so on
markers
rounded scissors

Letter of the Week

Celebrating a letter of the week invites children to learn the alphabet by sight and sound through creative play and art. Each week choose a different letter. Then have each child cut out that letter using an entire sheet of 8 ½" x 11" construction paper. Children can choose stickers, cut pictures from old magazines, or make original drawings of things that begin with the letter of the week. They can also glue small objects beginning with that letter onto their block letters, such as cotton balls, crayon pieces, clips, and so on.

Practice the letter sounds with the children. Have them keep sheets of paper next to their letters. Throughout the week, challenge them to write (or dictate) a list of as many words as possible that start with the letter of the week. Children can practice reading and sounding out the words as well.

Collages

You will need

felt
glue or paste
rounded scissors
scraps of material
yarn, ribbon, or string

Material Mania

Explore different textures with the children while they make material collages. Save old scraps of material, yarn, ribbon, and other items with interesting textures. Provide rounded scissors and invite children to cut various sizes and shapes to glue onto large pieces of felt.

You will need

clear plastic wrap
construction paper, crayons,
    markers, or paint
glue or paste
shoebox lids or other small lids
small paper bags
tape
treasures from nature, such as
    leaves, seeds, shells, or twigs

Nature Boxes

Collecting items for Nature Boxes is half the fun of this activity! Give each child a small paper bag. Tell children that you will be going on a nature hunt to collect items to make Nature Boxes. Explain that they may only collect items from the ground—they may not pick flowers, leaves, or twigs from plants or trees.

When you return from your nature hunt, provide each child with a shoebox lid or other small box lid for their creations (you may want to ask children to bring these from home). Have them cover the inside of their lids with construction paper and decorate with crayons, markers, or paint. Children can glue shells, leaves, twigs, seeds, or whatever treasures they found in nature to the inside of their lids. Help children stretch clear plastic wrap around the box lids to enclose their Nature Boxes. Then show them how to carefully tape the plastic to the back of the lids. Display children's creations around the room.

Collages

You will need

cardstock
dry noodles of various sizes and shapes
glue or paste

Noodlescape

Children are surprised at the variety of noodles available, as many are familiar with only spaghetti and macaroni. Provide a variety of dry noodles for children to make Noodlescapes. Children can glue the noodles in original designs onto pieces of cardstock.

Photo Quest

Instead of throwing out mediocre photographs, save them to create a Photo Quest memory book! Ask children to bring photographs from home that can be used for a collage. Then give each child several sheets of cardstock. Have children choose photos for each page of their books. They may want to crop and shape their photos before gluing them onto the cardstock. Then encourage children to draw pictures on each page of their books, incorporating the photos into their drawings. Help children bind their memory books by using a hole punch and tying the pages together with yarn or ribbon.

You will need

cardstock
glue or paste
hole punch
markers
photographs
rounded scissors
yarn or ribbon

Crafts

Invite children to create their own crafts with as little involvement from you as possible. Pride in their projects increases when children feel they are the true creators. Sometimes creating in a different environment sparks new ideas. While crafts are often thought of as an indoor activity, consider doing them outdoors. Outdoor workstations often make cleanup easier with a broom and hose.

You will need

aluminum foil
colored plastic wrap
permanent markers
pipe cleaners
rounded scissors
ruler

Aluminum Foil Sculptures

Children can create their own delicate, shimmering sculptures out of aluminum foil. Invite the children to explore folding, pinching, squeezing, and twisting pieces of foil into their own unique works of art. Or show them how to make foil dolls. First, help each child measure and cut a 20-inch sheet of foil and roll it into a 3-inch cone. Next, each child can pinch the cone in the center to create a waist for the doll. The bottom becomes a dress. Then have each child pinch half way between the waist and the top of the cone for a neck. He or she can press the foil above the neck into a ball for a head. Children can dress their dolls or decorate their sculptures by using colored plastic wrap over the foil. Then they can decorate their foil creations with colorful permanent markers.

16

Crafts

You will need

construction paper or fabric
crayons, markers, or paint
glue or paste
knife (for adult use only)
noodles, seeds, dried beans,
  glitter
recycled cans with plastic lids,
  such as coffee or powdered
  baby formula cans
rounded scissors

Coin Cans

Coin Cans are just the item to encourage children to save money! Have the children save cans with plastic lids. Help them measure, cut, and glue fabric or construction paper to fit around their cans. They can then glue lightweight items, such as noodles, seeds, dried beans, or glitter to the paper or fabric on the cans. Encourage children to use markers, crayons, and paint to add original designs. Cut a slit in each plastic lid large enough for coins to slip through.

Noodle Necklace

You and the children will want to make Noodle Necklaces again and again! Help children measure and cut pieces of string or yarn long enough to fit over their heads. Then show them how to wind tape around one end of a string to make a needle, so that they can thread the noodles more easily. Tie a knot around the first noodle threaded to hold the rest in place. Once children have finished threading the noodles, tie the two ends of the string together to complete the necklace. The necklaces are fun to keep or use as party favors.

As an extension to increase their math skills, have the children arrange the noodles by size and shape before they make their necklaces.

You will need

dry noodles with a hole
rounded scissors
string or yarn
tape

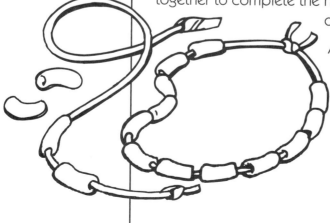

Crafts

You will need

acrylic or tempera paint
cookie cutters
cookie sheet
paintbrushes
plastic bags
plastic or butter knives
rolling pin

For the dough:

2 cups warm water
1 cup salt
⅔ cup oil
5 cups flour

Dough Figures

Invite children to bake their creations! Explain to the children that they will be making dough to play with, not eat. Place the dough ingredients on a table. Help children measure and mix the ingredients, being sure to mix the ingredients in the order here (children may need to add more flour while kneading the dough to achieve proper consistency). The recipe makes enough dough for 6 children.

Give each child a ball of dough and help him or her roll it out on a flat surface sprinkled with flour (so the dough won't stick). Then encourage children to use cookie cutters and plastic or butter knives to form works of art! Place their designs on a cookie sheet to bake at 300° F for half an hour to an hour, depending on the size and thickness of the dough figures. When ready, figures should be firm. After the dough cools, children can paint their figures with acrylic or tempera paint. Remember that these dough figures are not edible! To store unused dough, place it in a plastic bag, seal tightly, and store at room temperature.

Crafts

You will need

markers or crayons
nut cracker
nuts in the shells, such as
    almonds, peanuts, and
    walnuts

Nuts of the World

Help the children discover how many things they can make out of nutshells by turning snack time into an activity! Half a walnut shell can become a boat, a basket, or the body for a turtle. Peanut shells make great caterpillars. Almond shells turn into fun bugs. Place an assortment of nutshells on a table. Provide markers or crayons for children to draw details on the shells. You may also provide whole nuts and have children shell the nuts themselves. That way, they can eat the nuts as they create their nutshell art. Display the nutshell creations around the room.

Important note: Before you choose this activity, make sure none of the children are allergic to nuts.

You will need

glue gun or strong adhesive
markers or acrylic paint
miscellaneous tiny items to glue
    onto rocks
paintbrushes
smooth rocks of different sizes

Rock Sculptures

With the children, venture outside for a rock hunt. Encourage them to find smooth rocks of many sizes to turn into sculptures. Using a glue gun or strong adhesive, help them glue small rocks onto larger rocks to make animals, people, or interesting sculptures. Children can color their rock sculptures with markers or acrylic paint. If you have small art supplies on hand, encourage children to add finishing touches by gluing tiny items on their rocks for a custom look. Rock Sculptures can be used as toys, gifts, imaginary play, or accent pieces in their rooms.

Crafts

You will need

hole punch
iron
ironing board
newspaper
pieces of colored crayons
ruler
rounded scissors
small pencil sharpeners
string or yarn
waxed paper

Stained Glass Window

Save broken crayons and make Stained Glass Windows that shine brightly in the sun! Give children broken pieces of colored crayons and small pencil sharpeners. Have them sharpen their crayons over a sheet of newspaper, letting the crayon shavings fall on the paper. Next, help each child measure and cut two 12-inch squares of waxed paper. Cover an ironing board with newspaper. Then have each child place one square of waxed paper onto the newspaper. Each child can sprinkle the crayon shavings onto the waxed paper and then place a second sheet of waxed paper over the crayon shavings. Cover the waxed paper with another sheet of newspaper. With children, press the papers with a warm iron until the crayon shavings melt. Remove the waxed paper from between the newspapers and invite each child to trim the edges of his or her Stained Glass Window for a finished look. Help children use a hole punch to make holes. Thread strings through the holes to hang the creations from window frames in front of a sunny window.

Crafts

You will need

butcher paper
construction paper
craft sticks or recycled frozen fruit bar sticks
dough, clay, or putty
markers
rounded scissors
small toy cars and other village items

Traffic Jam

Traffic Jams offers hours of entertainment after road construction is complete. Using the illustrations here as a guide, show children how to draw road signs. While they draw and cut road signs out of construction paper, discuss the sign colors and shapes. Help children learn what each sign means. Then children can write (or dictate) the correct traffic rule for each sign.

Glue the finished signs to craft sticks or recycled frozen fruit bar sticks. Push the sticks into balls of dough, clay, or putty. Then show children how to draw roads on butcher paper and place the traffic signs along the way. To complete their town, children can find small village toys to use with their newly created roads and traffic signs. When their construction project is complete, toy cars are fun to maneuver through the town. Reinforce rules of the road while children are playing.

Greeting Cards

Children take pride in creating projects that family and friends will delight in receiving. Greeting cards are just that project. With a little direction, children can use their imaginations to create unique cards with a variety of materials. Each card can include a personal message from the child.

Chalk Cards

Using sheets of dark construction paper and a variety of colored chalks, invite children to create modern art masterpieces! The colored chalk almost glows on the dark construction paper. Have the children fold and cut their chalk designs into four pieces. Then have them fold four new sheets of construction paper in half and glue or paste chalk designs on the front of each of their four cards. To keep the chalk from rubbing off, spray children's finished drawings with aerosol hairspray.

Holiday Collage Cards

Holiday Collage Cards are festive and easy to make. Help the children choose colored sheets of paper to use for their holiday cards and fold their papers to the desired size. Show children how to glue small items on the front of their cards to represent the holiday they are celebrating. Old greeting cards, balloons, small decorations, wrapping paper, ribbon, and paper goods are items the children can cut and glue. Help them write (or dictate) a holiday message to put in the cards.

You will need

colored chalk
construction paper
glue or paste
hairspray
rounded scissors

You will need

balloons
construction paper
glue or paste
markers
old greeting cards or wrapping
    paper
paper goods
ribbons
rounded scissors
small decorations

Greeting Cards

Photo Cards

You will need

construction paper
glue or paste
markers
old photographs
rounded scissors

Give each child a sheet of construction paper to fold into a card. Then ask children to choose photos they want to design their cards around. They can crop the photos to the desired size and shape. Next, they need to place their photos on their cards and decide what pictures or designs they want to create around the photos. They can draw pictures or cut out designs, such as flowers, from construction paper. Using the illustration here, demonstrate how to cut flower petals from construction paper. After the children cut their petals, they can glue the petals to form flowers around their photos. Invite them to spiff up the cards by drawing around the flowers. Encourage children to think of other layout ideas using photographs.

Greeting Cards

You will need

construction paper
glue or paste
markers
rounded scissors
ruler

Pop-Up Cards

Many children like the detail of three-dimensional Pop-Up Cards. Have each child start with two sheets of construction paper that are the same size. Fold both sheets in half together lengthwise. Next, remove one of the folded sheets. On the middle of one fold, help the child measure and cut two ½-inch slits, one inch apart. Then, push out the middle portion between the two slits. The pushed out piece will eventually hold a small picture.

Show children how to glue the two sheets of paper together. Place glue around the four edges of the folded, but uncut, sheet of paper. Place the sheet with the cutout on top, being sure to pull out the pop-out section. After gluing the two sheets of paper together, open the card. Make sure the cut portion in the center of the fold is pulled out. Then invite each child to draw a small picture to glue on the front of the small pop-out portion of his or her card. Watch as children open and close their creations with gleeful pride. Encourage children to write (or dictate) a message and give their cards to someone special.

Greeting Cards

You will need

cardstock
envelopes
markers
rounded scissors

Puzzle Cards

It is a fun challenge to be on the receiving end of a Puzzle Card. Invite each child to draw an original picture on a piece of cardstock. Encourage each child to write (or dictate) a message and then sign his or her name. Help each child cut his or her cardstock into four or five puzzle pieces and place the puzzle pieces into an envelope to mail to a friend or relative. If a child wants the recipient to know who sent the card before it's put together, the child can include his or her name on the envelope.

You will need

construction paper
crayons
glue or paste
photographs
rounded scissors

Transfer Cards

Children often find it hard to believe that they are the creators of these special, almost magical Transfer Cards! Show children how to fold a sheet of construction paper in half vertically and color the inside left page completely with crayons. Then have each child fold his or her paper closed and, pushing hard, draw a picture with a pencil on the front cover. The drawing will transfer in color onto the inside right page. Invite children to write (or dictate) a message around their pictures.

Painting

Painting is how many children might first realize they have creative imaginations! Dressed in a smock, and with simple materials, children start with a blank slate and end with a masterpiece.

Gadget Stamp Painting

You will need

bowl or pie tin
construction paper
felt
sponges, bottle tops,
    feathers, twigs, or
    small rocks
tempera paint

Gadget Stamp Painting takes children one step further in becoming aware of their unlimited creativity. First, take them on a gadget hunt to find sponges, bottle tops, corks, and other unusual materials to use as painting instruments. Place a piece of felt in a plastic bowl and cover it with tempera paint to create a stamp pad effect. Using the found gadgets, show children how to ink their objects and then stamp away on colored construction paper.

Sponge Painting

You will need

construction paper
sharp scissors (for adult use
    only)
small containers
sponges
tempera paint

Using sharp scissors, cut sponges into interesting shapes, such as triangles, squares, or stars. Cover a table with newspaper, and place the sponge shapes and small containers of tempera paint on a table. Provide a larger container of water as well. Then have children dampen their sponges in the water, wring them out, and carefully dip them in tempera paint. Show children how to gently blot the shapes on sheets of paper to make interesting designs. Discuss the shapes that they chose and how their pictures would change if they used different shapes.

Painting

You will need

clothespins
construction paper
string
small containers
tempera paint

String Painting

String Painting is a unique method for children to create art. Place small containers of tempera paint on a table. Then invite children to dip pieces of string into the paint. Show children how to then clip the clothespins onto the strings and drag their tempera-dipped strings across paper to design works of art.

You will need

construction paper
cotton swabs
small containers
tempera paint

Swab Painting

Swab Painting helps children develop fine motor skills as they create pictures with their tiny painting instruments. Give each child a sheet of paper and a supply of cotton swabs. Place small containers of tempera paint on a table. Show children how to lightly dip the ends of the swabs into the paint and then use the swabs to design original artwork.

Painting

You will need

construction paper
felt
blunt knife or rounded scissors
knife (for adult use only)
potatoes, carrots, turnips,
    celery
small containers
tempera paint

Vegetable Printing

Potatoes, carrots, and turnips are just right to use for making vegetable prints. Cut the vegetables in half or in large pieces. Help the children make slices and other small cutouts with rounded scissors or blunt knives on one end of the cut vegetables. Then have them press the vegetables onto a piece of felt saturated with tempera paint and stamp a design with the vegetables onto paper. For a final addition, make several 1-inch slits at one end of a celery stalk. Have children hold the uncut end of the celery as the paintbrush handle to paint additional details with creative celery strokes.

Inside Days

It often seems that on days when children have to stay inside because of the weather, they have excess energy! Turn high-energy days into special memory days using these inside activities.

Bowling

You will need

blocks
rubber ball

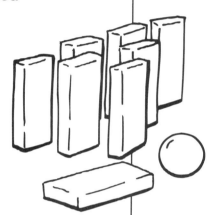

This indoor bowling game uses a combination of block building and ball rolling skills. Simply use children's blocks as "pins" and a rubber ball to knock them down. The fun is letting children set up the blocks in original patterns. Some children may line the blocks up, while others may group them or build towers to knock down. Encourage the children to start rolling the ball in a position not too far from the blocks. As they get better, have them move farther back. Join the fun yourself!

Box Creations

You will need

large, sturdy boxes
paint, markers, crayons, or chalk

After going on a box hunt at local stores, give children their own sturdy boxes and stand by for hours of endless entertainment! Invite children to decorate the outside of their boxes with paint, markers, crayons, and chalk. They may climb into the boxes and use them as houses, cars, trains, boats, or beds. Children will spend hours inventing various games, from peek-a-boo to train to house. Or they may simply tumble around in the boxes. They may choose to play as a group or individually. Sometimes a child may want to be alone, and a box can provide that place of solitude.

Inside Days

You will need

box or envelope
greeting cards, craft projects, or
*   collages*
postage

Care Packages

Making Care Packages can instill a sense of giving in children. Have them put together care packages filled with things they have created, such as art projects, homemade treats, and greeting cards. Each child can give or mail his or her  care package to someone special. Or you may, as a group, choose to send care packages to retirement homes or hospitals where they will be especially appreciated. Encourage children to choose to whom they would like to send their care packages.

You will need

three or four familiar objects

Memory Building

Children can build their memory skills while playing the Memory Building game. Place three or four large, familiar objects in a straight line, such as a spoon, a pen, a rock, and a stapler. To help children memorize the objects, have them say the name of each one aloud. Then, giving each child a turn, have one child cover his or her eyes while another child rearranges the objects. The child then uncovers his or her eyes and puts the objects in their original order. Increase the number of objects as the group seems ready.

Inside Days

You will need

construction paper
cupcakes or modeling dough
   cake
markers
small children's plates or a tea
   party set
stuffed animals
tempera paint

Party Time

Why wait an entire year for what is probably every child's favorite day of the year? Invite children to plan a birthday party for their favorite stuffed animals! With children, discuss a theme, such as a Winnie-the-Pooh party, a tea birthday party, and so on. Have the children make invitations from construction paper for themselves and the other stuffed animals. Party hats are fast and easy to make by simply taping together the two corners of the long side of a sheet of construction paper to form a cone. For more decorative hats, encourage children to decorate their hats with tempera paint or markers. Using their imaginations, they can make or find party favors to fit the theme. Next, have them make and decorate a modeling dough birthday cake or bake real cone cakes using the recipe on page 63. Finally, it's time to set the table with a tea party set and sing Happy Birthday!

Inside Days

You will need

dolls, stuffed animals, cars, trucks, or blocks
large sheet
table

Tent a Table

This fun, inventive activity offers a cozy spot for indoor play. Give children a sheet to drape over a table and their new playhouse is just the ticket to fantasyland! Add dolls and it becomes a house. Add cars and trucks and it becomes a garage. Add blocks and it becomes new construction. With a few suggestions from you, children actively create throughout the day.

You will need

tray
small items

Vanishing Objects

Place five or six small, recognizable objects on a tray. While the children sit in a circle, have them view the items on the tray. Then have them cover their eyes with their hands. Ask a child to remove one item from the tray. The other children open their eyes and try to guess which item vanished. The game continues until each child has a chance to remove an item. As children get used to the process, add more items to the tray. You'll be amazed at how much they remember!

Performance

It's amazing to see children who are often quiet or reserved come alive when performing. Putting on performances for themselves and others gives children an opportunity to show their talents as well as learn new ones.

Drama

Most children love to ham it up, and putting on these fun performances gives them the chance to do so in style! Your productions can be as simple or complex as you choose. A complete production can take up to a week, doing a different segment each day. One day work on the story, the next day work on costume and set design, then dress rehearsal complete with makeup, and finally, the final production. Children can perform their play for other children or family members. If a whole production seems like too much, Impromptu Shows (page 38) can take less than half an hour from start to finish.

Choose a Story

Children's imaginations often go wild when deciding on a story to perform. They may choose a story you have on hand or visit a library to choose a story or play. Choose a story with which children are familiar, such as *Stone Soup* by Marcia Brown (Simon & Schuster, 1997) or *Where the Wild Things Are* by Maurice Sendak (Harper Collins, 2000). You could even help children write or dictate an original play!

Choose Characters

Once you and the children have chosen the story, write the names of each character in the story on a slip of paper. Place the names in a large hat. Children can draw character parts out of the hat. Or you may choose to ask children to volunteer for the characters they want to play. If two children want the same part, it's back to the hat for a random decision, or you could double-cast and present the play twice!

You will need

book, play, or original story

You will need

book, play, or original story
hat
slips of paper

Drama

You will need

dress-up clothes
grocery bag
old clothes
paintbrushes
rounded scissors
tempera paint

Costume Designers

Explain to children that they can be costume designers! Discuss with children the appropriate costumes for each character. Then invite children to create costumes for their play. Ask children if they have dress-up clothes that would work for any of the characters. Bring in old clothes, hats, and scarves for children to use for costumes. Children can also make costumes. For example, using grocery bags, help children cut holes for their heads and holes for each arm. With tempera paint, children can create wonderful paper bag costumes, such as white rabbits, brown mice, or black bugs.

You will need

8½" x 11" colored paper
glitter glue
hole punch
rounded scissors
string

Face Mask Designers

Many children like to dress in disguises, but don't want their faces totally covered. These face masks leave children's eyes, noses, and mouths exposed. Have the children fold sheets of paper in half vertically or horizontally. Then they can draw half of a shape on the fold, such as a half of a heart, star, pine tree, or pumpkin. Next help children cut out the designs on the folds. When they unfold their papers, the whole design will appear, cut out from the middle of the paper. They can use glitter glue to dress up the outside edges around the shape. Then have children use a hole-punch to make holes for a string on the short ends of their masks. Children can tie the strings around their heads, leaving their faces showing through the shapes!

Drama

You will need

construction paper
cotton balls
glue or paste
pipe cleaners
rounded scissors
ruler
stapler or tape

Hat Designers

Hats may be the only costumes you need! First, help each child measure and cut two 3" x 11" strips of construction paper to form bands. Staple or tape each band to fit the child's head. Children can then personalize their headbands to fit their characters. For example, if you decide to do *Where the Wild Things Are* by Maurice Sendak (Harper Collins, 2000), you can make rabbit ears by measuring and cutting two 1" x 4" pink strips of construction paper and gluing cottonballs down the center. Then glue the strips onto the headband. To make mouse ears, cut and glue brown ovals onto the headband. To make curly bug ears, wind pipe cleaners around a pencil, then pull the pipe cleaners off and glue them onto the headband.

You will need

eyebrow pencils
face paint
makeup
wet wipes, cold cream, or tissues

Makeup Designers

Many children enjoy dabbling in makeup! Use face paints to make the children up to look like their characters. You can also use inexpensive makeup as an alternative to store-bought face paint. Help children use eyebrow pencils to create features, such as whiskers or spots for animals, and mustaches, freckles, or eyelashes for human characters. When the production is over, children can remove makeup with wet wipes or cold cream and tissues.

Drama

You will need

*cardstock, butcher paper, or
    cardboard boxes*
*kitchen utensils, small furniture,
    toys, or other common items*
markers or tempera paint
paintbrushes

You will need

easel
markers
posterboard
tape

Set Designers

Set design can be as simple or elaborate as you choose. Have the children use butcher paper as a backdrop, cardboard boxes for dimension, and tempera paint for color and detail. Children can paint the backdrop with houses, trees, or anything appropriate to the story. Encourage children to go on a prop hunt at school or at home for common items, such as kitchen utensils, small furniture, or toys to fit the story line.

Playbill

A playbill for your production is the final touch. Using a large sheet of posterboard, write the name of the play at the top. Then children can draw a picture depicting the story they are presenting. Write the name of each job in the production on the playbill, including writers, actors, singers, set designers, costume designers, and so on. Then ask each child to write his or her name under each job that they did: story writer, actor, singer, dancer, costume designer, makeup artist, set designer, or audience. Make sure everyone who works diligently on the stage or behind the scenes puts his or her name on the playbill. Then display the playbill on an easel, if available, or tape the playbill to a wall for all to see.

Drama

You will need

construction paper
crayons or markers
glitter glue or stickers

Invitations

The children's dramatic production can be for themselves, other children, or family and friends. If they want to invite others, offer a variety of basic art materials for children to use to create simple invitations to their production. Instruct them to include the title of the show, date, time, and location of the performance on the invitations.

You will need

dress-up clothes
furniture
toys

Impromptu Shows

If you don't want to create a complete production, an Impromptu Show might be just the ticket. With the children, choose a familiar story. Assign parts by having children draw characters' names from a hat. If there aren't enough parts for everyone, children can be flowers, trees, or the audience to laugh, clap, and cheer. Use readily available items, such as dress-up clothes, furniture, and toys. Remember that there is no rehearsal. Encourage children to act out the story as they know it. Have the children who were extras in this show be first to pick parts for the next show.

Puppets

Puppets serve a multitude of purposes. They are not only a creative project, but when complete, become a tool for children to express their feelings. Also, children who are reluctant to speak in a group may be less shy when using puppets. Invite children to act out their favorite stories and books with puppets. Or challenge them to try their hands at writing and performing original productions!

You will need

construction paper
crayons or markers
glue or paste
paper lunch bag
rounded scissors
yarn, fabric scraps, or buttons

Bag Puppets

Bag Puppets are fun to make and lend themselves to a great game of pretend. Flatten paper lunch bags and have the children slip their hands into the inside folds. The flat bottom of each bag becomes the head. The head moves as the children's fingers move back and forth within the bag. The moving fold resembles the mouth. Have the children cut eyes, noses, and mouths out of construction paper and glue them onto the bags. Or they can draw faces with crayons or markers. Yarn works well for hair, fabric scraps are good for clothes, and buttons make excellent eyes.

Picture Puppets

Picture Puppets are quick and easy to make. Have the children cut and shape people and animals from extra family photographs. Or children can cut images of people and pets from old magazines, catalogs, or greeting cards. Then have them glue their cutouts onto craft sticks to use as puppets. When children finish their puppets, the show begins!

You will need

craft sticks or recycled frozen
   fruit bar sticks
extra family photographs,
   recycled catalogs,
   magazines, or greeting cards
glue or paste
rounded scissors

Puppets

You will need

12-inch squares of fabric
6-inch plastic foam balls
buttons
craft or recycled frozen fruit bar
  sticks
glue or paste
markers
ruler
yarn

Plastic Foam Puppets

Plastic Foam Puppets are durable and easy to assemble. Children can use as much or as little detail as they want. Give each child a 6-inch plastic foam ball for a head. Children can use glue to attach buttons for the eyes and nose, and yarn for hair. Invite them to use markers to draw faces. After children finish the faces, help them put craft sticks in the middle of 12-inch squares of fabric and then push the sticks and fabric into the plastic foam heads. The sticks under the fabric make handles for children to easily hold during a dramatic presentation.

You will need

box cutter or scissors (for adult
  use only)
chairs or wardrobe box
couch
crayons, markers, or paint
sheet or tablecloth

Puppet Theater

Quick and easy puppet theaters can be almost anywhere—peeking from the side of a doorway or reaching over a couch or chair. Invite children to drape a sheet across two chairs placed on either side of a doorway. Or use a recycled wardrobe box to create an instant theater. Place the wardrobe box flat on the floor and cut out a window in the upper half of one of the long sides. Place the wardrobe upright and invite children to decorate the box, then hop into it to give their show!

Puppets

You will need

puppets
theater

Puppet Show

After assembling their puppets and making a theater, the children are ready for their Puppet Show! Most children may express an interest in creating an original show, rather than recreating a book or play. Some children may want to perform alone, others in pairs. A group show where each child has a part is also an option. Encourage children to present their shows to each other, or invite family and friends!

Storytelling

Most children enjoy telling stories, especially about things that happen to them. It doesn't seem to matter who is reading the book, telling the story, or even if there is a guest speaker; they want to add their experiences. The activities below give children an opportunity to jump in whenever they feel their experiences or stories are appropriate.

Flannelboard Stories

Telling stories using flannelboards is a colorful, tangible form of storytelling that involves as few or as many children as you want. Cut an 18" x 24" sheet of heavy corrugated cardboard. To make a flannelboard, cover the cardboard with felt and secure it firmly with staples and tape. With the children, cut figures and shapes out of felt. Or the children can cut out magazine or catalogue pictures to glue to precut felt shapes. Then have children share their tales by placing the figures on the flannelboard as they tell their stories.

Record a Story

Recording stories and then listening to their voices provides hours of entertainment for children. Have the children record their own voices while reading a story, retelling their favorite story, or making up an original story. Children can vary their speaking voices from a whisper to a shout or from speaking quickly to slowly. These recordings make great keepsakes.

Storytelling

© Fearon Teacher Aids FE11053

You will need

children's story book

Story Starters

Begin Story Starters by sitting with the children in a cozy spot. Begin by reading a sentence or even a scene from a book. Challenge children to then continue the story, making it up as they go along. Or you can begin with a phrase and have the children use the phrase to begin a story. Then listen as children's creativity explodes!

Some open-ended phrases you can begin with are:

I want to be . . .
If I saw an alien, I would . . .
If I could have anything for dinner, I would have . . .
If I could go anywhere, I would go . . .
If the lights went out at night, I would . . .
If I found $100.00, I would . . .

You will need

ball of yarn

Web Tales

Web Tales help children learn more about each other and gain confidence in speaking in a group. Have the children sit in a circle. Pose simple questions, such as: What is your favorite color? What is your favorite sport? Then move on to the more complex questions: What is your address? What is your favorite story? Who is your favorite role model? Why? Before you ask each question, give one child a ball of yarn. The child with the yarn has the option of answering the question or saying "pass." After answering or saying "pass," the child holds onto the end of the yarn and rolls the ball across the circle to another child. After answering or passing, that child holds onto the yarn and rolls the ball across the circle to a different child. So goes the webbing until each child has a turn to answer or pass and the Web Tale is complete.

Storytelling

Songs and Fingerplays

Speaking in front of a group can increase self-confidence. But for some children, singing is a beginning. Start with the old standards—many children like singing familiar songs. Include, if possible, finger, hand, and whole body movement to teach rhythm, release energy, exercise the body, and show the importance of body language. For most of these songs and fingerplays, you will need only fingers and voices to join in!

Old Standards

Many of the children know the words and movements to many old standards like the ones here. Use these with the children or add a twist to each as you sing and fingerplay!

Eensy Weensy Spider

This familiar song and fingerplay is fun to sing in the spring when it's rainy and the bugs and spiders are out, or around Halloween when spooky spiders appear. Talk about spiders and bugs after you sing the song.

> The eensy weensy spider went up the waterspout.
> Down came the rain and washed the spider out.
> Out came the sun and dried up all the rain.
> And the eensy weensy spider went up the spout again.

Old MacDonald Had a Farm

Children enjoy singing "Old MacDonald Had a Farm" while making different animal sounds. Have each child decide what animal he or she wants to sing about before the song begins. With children, decide what order they will sing about their animals.

> (Everyone sings)
> Old MacDonald had a farm,
> E I E I O
> (One child sings)
> And on that farm, he had some chicks.
> E I E I O
>
> (Chorus)
> With a cluck, cluck here
> And a cluck, cluck there.
> Here a cluck,
> There a cluck,
> Everywhere a cluck, cluck.
> Old MacDonald had a farm,
> E I E I O
>
> Repeat verse using:
> Duck—quack (one child sings out).
> Turkey—gobble (one child sings out).
> Pig—oink (one child sings out).
> Cow—moo (one child sings out).
> Horse—neigh (one child sings out).

Storytelling

Pop Goes the Weasel

On the days when children seem to have an abundance of energy, "Pop Goes the Weasel" is an opportunity for them to burn it up!

> All around the cobbler's bench,
> The monkey chased the weasel,
> The monkey thought it was all in fun,
> POP goes the weasel.
> A penny for a spool of thread,
> A penny for a needle,
> That's the way the money goes,
> POP! Goes the weasel.

Rain Rain Go Away

Turn a rainy day into a sunny day as the children take turns substituting their names into the song and waving the rain away.

> Rain, rain, go away,
> Come again another day.
> Little Johnny wants to play,
> Rain, rain, go away.

Row Row Row Your Boat

Children can row make-believe boats as they sing "Row Row Row Your Boat" in a round.

> Row, row, row your boat
> Gently down the stream.
> Merrily, merrily, merrily
> Life is but a dream.

Twinkle Twinkle Little Star

Talk about the night sky before singing "Twinkle Twinkle Little Star" with children. Sing this song as they make moons and stars for *Goodnight Moon* (page 89).

> Twinkle, twinkle little star.
> How I wonder what you are.
> Up above the world so high,
> Like a diamond in the sky.
> Twinkle, twinkle little star.
> How I wonder what you are.

Storytelling

You will need

sign language chart

ABC Sign Language

Children can explore another way to communicate using sign language! Challenge the children to sing the ABC's while following the sign language chart. After singing the ABC's, they can practice spelling their names or other words using sign language.

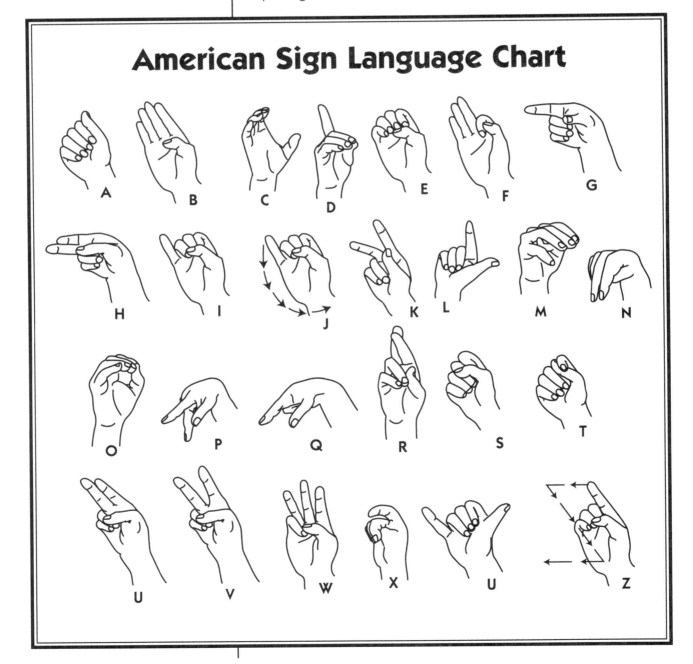

American Sign Language Chart

A B C D E F G

H I J K L M N

O P Q R S T

U V W X U Z

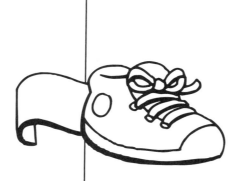

Movement

Movement improves children's gross motor development and coordination, and keeps them mentally and physically fit. Help children understand that movement—whether it be exercise, indoor or outdoor games, dance, and so on—is important for growth. When children are active, they breathe harder and their hearts beat faster, which develops stronger bodies and minds.

Exercise

When it comes to exercise, adults often assume children are getting enough because children are naturally active. But that may not be the case. Get children moving with these fun, physical games. For many of these activities, you will not need any materials.

You will need

music
scarves
scraps of material
streamers

Creative Dance

Give children streamers, scarves, and scraps of material, and you may be surprised at their performing talents and movement! Play music and invite them to dance and move their bodies and props quickly or slowly, depending on the tempo of the music.

Growing Tree

This activity gives children an opportunity to stretch their muscles. Have children pretend they are seeds by curling into balls on the ground. Explain that water and sunlight make seeds grow. Ask children to imagine that they are being watered and slowly growing into trees. First, they poke their hands up to simulate a sprouting seed. Then they slowly move to a standing position. Show them how to wave their arms high in the air as if they are branches swaying in the wind. Then have the children decide if the wind is blowing strongly or gently.

Exercise

Helicopter

Here's a chance for children to fly off into a world of make-believe! To become helicopters, have the children stretch their arms straight above their heads and rotate them around and around. Then have the children reverse the direction of their arms. As they're flying away, ask everyone where their helicopters are going, why, and when they will be back.

Jumping Beans

Get children moving and their blood pumping fast! Invite them to pretend to be jumping beans and jump on both feet from one designated spot to another and back again. Provide lively music as they jump.

You will need

balls of various sizes

Kick It, Roll It, Bounce It

Have the children experiment with ball handling and improve their hand-eye coordination whether they choose to kick, roll, bounce, throw, or hit a ball. Encourage children to throw the balls against an outside wall, or kick a ball back and forth with another child. They can form teams and play games as well, such as kickball, soccer, or four-square.

Exercise

Long and Short

While playing Long and Short, children learn to estimate size, length, and distance. Have them spread out and stand side by side in a line. Stand several feet in front of children. Spread your arms out wide to indicate the concept of "long" and bring your hands close together to indicate "short." Children take the same size steps forward as you indicate with your hands. The first child to touch you can be the next leader.

Zero, Blast Off!

This is a great exercise for generating enthusiasm! Count backward from 10 down to one. As you count aloud, have the children slowly move from a standing to a squatting position, so that they are all the way down to the floor by the time you reach number one. Tell children that when you say the words, "Zero, Blast Off!" they are to jump up as high as they can, as if they were rockets blasting off. Try counting at different speeds and have the children match the speed of their movements with your counting. Invite them to join you in shouting, "Zero, Blast Off!"

50

Indoor Active Play

Take organized indoor play one step beyond crafts, books, and board games. These unique games improve social and leadership skills. Using their creativity, children can modify or expand the games as they play.

You will need

index cards or paper
pencils

Address Hunt

This fun activity helps children learn where they live. Help them write (or dictate) their names, addresses, and phone numbers on individual index cards. If only a few children are playing, they can write relative's names on cards, too. Place the cards around the room so they are visible. Send the children on a hunt for their own cards. As they find their cards, ask children to take turns reading, chanting, or singing the information to you.

Animal Pantomime

Children can make more animal sounds than seems possible! Have the children sit in a circle. Then choose a child to act out an animal without talking. If no one guesses the animal, ask the child to make the appropriate animal sound. After someone guesses correctly, everyone makes the animal sound. Then the child who guessed correctly gets the next chance to pantomime an animal.

Indoor Active Play

You will need

chair
stuffed animal or book

Cat and Mouse

Cat and Mouse is a quiet game, except for the giggles! Choose one child to be the cat. The cat sits on a chair about fifteen feet away from the other children and covers his or her eyes. The cat's back is toward the other players. The cat's mouse—a stuffed animal or small book—"hides" behind the cat's chair. Silently choose one child by pointing to him or her. The selected child sneaks up to the cat and tries to touch the mouse without the cat hearing. If the cat hears someone coming, he or she turns around and says, "Meow!" Then the player goes back to the other children and another child has a chance to outsmart the cat and touch the mouse. If successful, this child is the next cat.

My Favorites

Usually children like to share things about themselves, so create a game with them as the stars! Ask the children if they like a specific thing. If they answer yes, then they must do what you tell them to do. For example, ask children if they like to eat ice cream. If any of the children say yes, tell those children to run in place. Ask if their favorite color is red. If some say yes, tell those children to jump up and down. Ask if they have a dog. If some say yes, tell them to touch their elbows. Or ask if they are scared of monsters. If some say yes, tell them to wave the monsters away. If the answer is no, they remain still. This activity gets children moving, reinforces parts of the body, and lets children share facts about themselves.

52

Indoor Active Play

Kids Say

Kids Say, a variation of Simon Says, is a valuable game that teaches children to lead, follow, and listen. Give each child an opportunity to lead the group, while others listen and follow the directions. Standing across the room, the leader gives a direction, such as, "(leader's name) says touch your nose." The other children follow the direction every time it is preceded by the leader's name. If the children follow the direction correctly, they may take one step forward. If the leader does not say his or her name before giving a direction, the others must remain still. If someone incorrectly follows the direction, that child must go back one step. After a few turns, the child closest to the leader becomes the next leader.

Kitty in a Chair

This game gives children an opportunity to run around indoors! Help the children scatter chairs around the room. There should be one less chair than the number of children playing. Choose one child to stand in the middle of the room to be the kitty, while the others choose a chair to sit in. When the kitty in the middle says, "Kitty wants a chair," all children, including the kitty in the middle, run to different chairs. The child left without a chair becomes the kitty in the middle. Make sure no one is the kitty more than three or four times in a row.

You will need

chairs

Indoor Active Play

You will need

furniture
Hula-Hoop
string or yarn
timer or watch with a second hand

Obstacle Course

Give children the opportunity to learn to work as a team as you help them set up an Obstacle Course with available furniture. Have children consider going over a chair, under a table, around a plant, or in a Hula-Hoop. They could even balance on a line or other obstacle. Before they try the obstacle course, place a string along the way showing the path to follow. After they've had a few practice rounds, remove the string. If appropriate, show children how to time each other. Children often repeat an obstacle course over and over, trying to improve their time.

You will need

peanuts in the shell
small paper bags

Peanut Hunt

Peanut Hunt is a simple game that is easy to set up, yet always a hit! Before beginning, make sure that none of the children are allergic to peanuts. While the children are in a separate area, hide the peanuts. Then give each child a small paper bag and encourage the group to begin their great hunt! Children can take turns re-hiding the peanuts they didn't eat, then you can send them off on another peanut hunt.

Indoor Active Play

Group Games

There are a number of well known games to play indoors that are active and fun! These games can be played over and over again and the children will not get tired of them. Play these games as you know them, or add a twist to make the games more interesting!

Duck, Duck, Goose

Encourage children to make their own words for the game, like "Ball, Ball, Bounce" or "Tap, Tap, Run." You can also extend this game by working out a path that the old goose and new goose run, perhaps around a chair and a table.

Follow the Leader

The leader can walk, jump, hop, crawl, skip, or run. Challenge leaders to come up with new ideas, such as singing a song, stopping to read a story with each child reading part of the story, and so on.

Hide and Seek

Sardines is a challenging variation of Hide and Seek. One child hides first, as the rest of the group closes their eyes and counts to twenty. Then the group goes in search of It. When a child finds It, he or she quietly joins him or her while the others continue their search. As each child finds the growing group of Sardines, he or she joins them. The last person to find the group is the new It. This game is a challenge for children to remain quiet as well as to find a hiding spot with room for everyone!

Hot Potato

Challenge children by having them say a word that begins with a specific letter before they can pass on the hot potato.

Musical Chairs

Play this game in slow motion, playing very slow music as children move to the beat to find chairs.

Outdoor Play

Outdoor play not only burns up excess energy, but also improves gross and fine motor skills. It can be a time for group or individual play and a time to invent new games or play old ones. It should also be a time that is fun for all.

Box Basketball

Help children line up differently sized boxes at various distances from a beginning point. Then invite children to try their hand at Box Basketball! Show children how to stand behind the beginning point and throw a ball into each of the boxes. Children can take turns at each box. Depending on how easily the ball goes in and stays in, they may want to move the boxes accordingly.

Beanbag Toss

Provide different colors of chalk and invite children to draw targets on the sidewalk. The targets can be of any shape or design. Children should mark a place by their targets where players should stand. Children can throw beanbags at the targets. Move the standing marker closer or farther away as the games continue. If there are a number of drawn targets on the sidewalk, children can go from one to another in order to see how many they can get in a row.

If beanbags are not available, children can quickly make them by stuffing dried beans into small plastic bags. Be sure the bags are tightly sealed or the beans will fly everywhere!

You will need

ball
boxes bigger than the ball

You will need

beanbags or beanbag stuffed
*   dolls or animals*
chalk
dried beans
plastic bags

Outdoor Play

Road Construction

Have the children use sidewalk chalk to draw roads and towns on a hard surface outside. Provide toy cars, trucks, blocks, and other items for children to use to create a small village. Then encourage them to go to town!

You will need

blocks or children's building materials
sidewalk chalk
small village toys, cars, or trucks

Squirt

Help children fill clean, empty plastic squirt bottles with water. Then invite them to find appropriate things outside to squirt with water, such as outside walls, sidewalks, leaves, grass, and so on. Squirting is fun for children as they watch objects change color when the water hits them and then evaporates. If possible, children can put on raincoats or bathing suits and squirt themselves or each other!

You will need

clean squirt bottles
water

Outdoor Play

You will need

bucket or pails
large clean paintbrushes

Water Painting

Painting with water gives children great freedom. Have the children help you fill buckets or pails with water. Then show them how to dip large clean paintbrushes into the water and paint every waterproof object in sight. Water painting can be as fulfilling as painting with paint, especially if the objects are dirty. Children can watch the dirt vanish with each stroke. Encourage children to paint designs or play Tic Tac Toe before the water dries on a cemented area.

You will need

large boxes
riding toys, such as tricycles,
  scooters, cars, or trucks
sheets
small furniture
toys

Wheel Toy Village

Show the children how to create a village out of boxes, small furniture, and toys. You can also provide large sheets to drape over furniture to make houses or store fronts. When their village is complete, children can ride wheel toys through the village. While each child waits for his or her turn on a wheel toy, he or she can work in a service station or car wash; be a storekeeper or a parking lot attendant; serve as a police officer giving directions or tickets; and so on. Rotate children so everyone tries out each position. Don't worry about having enough toys for children to ride. Rather, make it fun to share and wait for a turn.

Responsibility

Children can learn responsibility through activities that allow them to perform necessary jobs and take pride in doing them. Cooking and gardening are ways in which children learn to be responsible for simple, interesting tasks as they create recipes and tend to their own garden!

Cooking

Cooking is an excellent way for children to learn math concepts without realizing it! While they are pouring and mixing, they learn fractions, measurements, the difference between more or less, and shapes. It's easy to understand why cooking is a favorite pastime for children; they like choosing recipes, mixing, pouring, and, of course, tasting! They even like washing and drying dishes, wiping counters, and sweeping the floor. Before children begin cooking, check for food allergies and make sure they always wash their hands.

Cheese Dogs

Children can make their own Cheese Dogs and learn about shapes at the same time! Point out each shape or concept as the children work with all the items in the recipe.

Have the children wash their hands. Give one refrigerated crescent dough triangle to each child. Help them unroll the dough, and cut the square cheese slices into two triangles with plastic knives. Invite each child to eat one of the triangle slices immediately and  place the other cheese triangle on top of the dough. Then have the children roll their round hot dogs into the middle of their cheese dough and place their Cheese Dogs on a cookie sheet. Bake at 350° F for 12 to 15 minutes or until crescent rolls brown.

You will need

cookie sheet
hot dogs
plastic knives
pre-sliced American cheese
  squares
refrigerated crescent roll dough

Cooking

You will need

9" x 13" pan
blunt or plastic knife
double boiler (or access to a microwave oven)
large wooden or plastic spoon
measuring cups and spoons
spatula
waxed paper

For cereal candy:

2¼ cups melted semisweet chocolate bits
4 cups unsweetened cereal of your choice
¼ cup dried fruits of your choice
½ cup marshmallows
¼ cup nuts of your choice

Cereal Candy

Cereal Candy is an alternative to cupcakes or cookies for a group treat! Have the children wash their hands. Invite children to measure and pour chocolate bits into a double boiler or a pan that can be used in the microwave. Carefully melt the chocolate. Chocolate burns easily, so keep an eye on it. Then have children add the cereal and optional ingredients to the melted chocolate and mix well. To make individual servings, have children drop the mixture by teaspoons onto waxed paper. After the mixture is cool, children can make the mixture into shapes, animals, or other designs with their hands. Or you may choose to make cereal bars, spreading the mixture with a spatula or spoon in a greased 9" x 13" pan. Cool and cut into about 24 bars.

Cooking

You will need

cookie cutters
cookie sheet
large mixing bowl
large wooden or plastic spoon
measuring cups and spoons
plastic knives
rolling pin

For the cookies:
1 cup soft butter
1 cup brown sugar
1 egg
1 tablespoon vanilla
3½ cups flour

frosting (recipe on page 63)
sprinkles or other candy
   toppings

Vanilla Cookies

Vanilla Cookies are easy to make and an old time favorite! Have the children wash their hands. Then help the children measure and stir the butter and brown sugar until smooth. Next, help them crack the egg and mix in the vanilla. Children can gradually add flour and stir. With a rolling pin, help children roll the dough out on a floured surface to ¼-inch thickness. Then children can either cut cookies from the dough with cookie cutters or shape the dough into letters and numbers, and place on a greased cookie sheet. Bake at 350° F for 10 minutes. While the cookies cool, have the children make frosting from the recipe on page 63. After spreading the frosting on the cookies, children can decorate cookies with sprinkles and other fun toppings for true works of art! The recipe makes about 3 dozen cookies.

Cooking

You will need

*cake mix and ingredients listed
  on package*
cookie sheet
flat bottom ice-cream cones
frosting
large mixing bowl
large wooden or plastic spoon
measuring cups and spoons
sprinkles

Cone Cakes

Cone Cakes are a treat for children to make because they bake their cakes in edible pans! Have the children wash their hands. Help the children measure and mix the cake batter according to package directions. Then help each child fill a flat-bottomed cone two-thirds full with the batter. If they put in too much or too little batter, the cones won't have nicely rounded tops. Place cones upright on a cookie sheet. Bake at temperature and time indicated on package for cupcakes. After the Cone Cakes cool, give each child a serving of frosting (recipe below) and some sprinkles. Often, children enjoy frosting, decorating, and admiring their creations more than eating them!

Frosting

Have the children wash their hands. Then help the children measure and pour all the ingredients into a bowl and stir and stir and stir!

You will need

large mixing bowl
large wooden or plastic spoon
measuring spoons

For the frosting:

1 cup powdered sugar
¼ teaspoon salt
½ teaspoon vanilla
*1½ tablespoons cream, milk, or
  water*
food coloring (optional)

Cooking

You will need

cookie sheet
cheese grater (optional)
English muffin
mozzarella cheese
spaghetti or pizza sauce
toaster
various toppings, such as bell
    pepper, ham, mushrooms,
    olives, onion, pepperoni, or
    pineapple

You will need

paper cups
pot, popcorn popper, or
    access to a microwave

For the popcorn:
butter (optional)
cooking oil
paper cups
Parmesan cheese
popcorn
salt

Individual Pizzas

Making Individual Pizzas gives children the opportunity to make their own pizzas just the way they like them! Have the children wash their hands. Give each child one half of a toasted English muffin. Pass a jar of spaghetti or pizza sauce with a spoon so each child can scoop and spread the amount of sauce he or she wants on the muffin. The amount of sauce isn't critical, as long as it's not running off the muffin. Next comes the cheese. It's best to buy pre-grated cheese, but some children may want to grate the cheese themselves. Supervision is important so they don't grate their knuckles. Show children how to place an appropriate amount of cheese on their pizzas. Then give them the option of selecting other toppings, such as olives, ham, pepperoni, pineapple, onion, mushrooms, or bell pepper. Have the children place their pizzas on a cookie sheet. Bake at 350° F for 7 to 10 minutes or until the cheese melts. Remind children to let their pizzas cool before eating.

Popcorn

Popcorn is easy to make and tastes so good! Children enjoy watching and listening to it pop in the microwave, in a pot on a stove, or in a popcorn popper. Give each child a paper cup to fill halfway with popcorn. Children can sprinkle their popcorn with Parmesan cheese or salt. If you would like, melt butter in a pan and help children pour a little bit on their popcorn.

No-Bake Cooking

With these no fuss, no muss recipes, there's no more worries about hot stoves or burned fingers and tongues! The recipes are easy, and you don't need a microwave, stove, or electric fry pan. The children can make their dishes from beginning to end at an inside or outside cooking center. Before starting, check for food allergies and make sure children always wash their hands. If someone is allergic to an ingredient or if you want to change the flavor of a dish, discuss what to add or delete.

Ants on a Log

Ants on a Log are imaginative, nutritious, and delicious! Have the children wash their hands. Help the children separate, wash, and cut celery sticks into 4-inch pieces. Give them blunt or plastic knives to spread peanut butter, cream cheese, or soft cheese inside the celery sticks. Then give children raisins to place in a row on top, as if they are ants walking on a log. They can then enjoy eating their masterpieces!

You will need

blunt or plastic knives
celery sticks
peanut butter, soft cheese, or
  cream cheese
raisins

Juice Pops

Juice Pops are healthy cold treats for a hot day! Have the children wash their hands. With the children, pour juice or flavored yogurt into individual paper cups. The yogurt will taste more like creamy ice cream. Next, cover each cup with aluminum foil. Have each child poke a craft stick through the center of the foil into the juice or yogurt. Then place the cups in the freezer. After the Juice Pops freeze, take the children outside where they can remove the foil, tear off the paper cups, and dive into their Pops!

You will need

aluminum foil
juice or flavored yogurt
plastic spoons or craft sticks
small paper cups

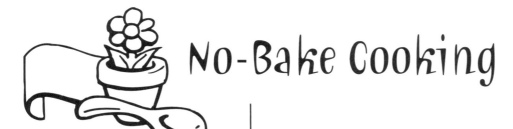

No-Bake Cooking

You will need

cookie sheet
food processor
mixing bowl
measuring cups

For raisin nut rolls:
1 ½ cups raisins
½ cup salted almonds

You will need

large wooden or plastic spoon
mixing bowl
measuring cups and spoons

For the peanut butter balls:
4 tablespoons peanut butter
3 tablespoons honey
½ cup non-fat powdered milk
*¼ cup dry non-sugar coated
    cereal flakes*

Raisin Nut Rolls

Raisin Nut Rolls are a snack with a creative twist! Have the children wash their hands. Help the children measure and combine the raisins and almonds and place in a food processor. Run the food processor until the almonds and raisins are a thick consistency. Next, carefully transfer the mixture into a bowl. Give each child a portion of the mixture and invite them to begin molding interesting shapes. Chill their designs on a cookie sheet in the refrigerator, or they can eat them on the spot!

Peanut Butter Balls

Have the children wash their hands. Help children measure and mix the peanut butter and honey in a large mixing bowl. Then children can slowly add non-fat dry milk and mix well. After mixing, show children how to form 16 Peanut Butter Balls by rolling the dough between their hands. Then have them roll the balls in dry cereal flakes. Chill until firm. After chilling, children can make peanut butter snowmen by placing one ball atop another and "gluing" them together with a couple of drops of honey.

No-Bake Cooking

You will need

dry ingredients, such as cereal,
   chocolate-covered candy,
   coconut chips, croutons,
   dried fruits, granola,
   marshmallows, nuts,
   popcorn, or pretzels
small serving bowls

Trail Mix

Every time children make Trail Mix, they can change the recipe depending upon what ingredients are available or what they want in it! Help the children pour a variety of ingredients from the list to the left into separate serving bowls. Then give the children their own empty bowls and invite them to make their own special Trail Mix by selecting from the various ingredients. Discuss how healthy Trail Mix is before they add marshmallows or chocolate. Have them taste their Trail Mix before they add sweets, then after. Talk about the taste difference.

Indoor Gardening

Indoor gardening brings greenery, flowers, and vegetables inside during every month of the year! Carefully explain and delegate responsibilities to the children. Then watch the children blossom as they fulfill their indoor gardening tasks.

Avocado Tree

Invite the children to sprout avocado trees that could give years of shade! Give each child an avocado seed. Or, you may want to have children work in small groups of two or three and sprout an avocado seed together. Have children clean the avocado seeds with water. Push four toothpicks into a circular position about halfway down each avocado seed. Then place the rounded end of each seed in a small glass of water, resting the toothpicks on the rim of a glass. The water level should remain almost up to the toothpicks. Have the children check the water levels periodically, adding water when necessary.

Keep the prepared seeds in a cool, dark area, such as a closet, until the children see some growth, which is usually in two to four weeks. Then place the sprouting seeds in a sunny area. Children like watching the bottom of the seeds sprout roots, followed by leaves on top. After you and the children have seen some good growth, invite the children to plant the sprouted seeds outside, making sure they allow for growing room. Their small avocado seeds may grow into large shade trees that may bear avocados if the climate is right and other avocado trees are close by to provide pollination.

You will need

avocado seeds
small glasses
toothpicks
water

Indoor Gardening

You will need

bowl 5 to 6 inches in diameter
pebbles or marbles
small bowls
tulips, crocus, paper whites, or
   melange bulbs
water

You will need

sponges
grass seed
saucers
water

Bulb in a Bowl

Give each child a small bowl, a flower bulb, and pebbles or marbles. Have the children fill their bowls ¾ full with pebbles or marbles. Then help them carefully push their bulbs into the pebbles, keeping the point of the bulbs up. Next, have the children add enough water to cover the bottom third of the bulbs. Their bulbs must be kept out of direct sunlight until they begin to root. The rooting process can take several weeks.

Encourage children to check to make sure the bottom third of their bulbs remain under water at all times. After the rooting process begins, they can move their bulb bowls to indirect sunlight and watch as stems sprout and flowers bloom!

Grass Garden

A Grass Garden inside? Yes! Give each child a sponge and have him or her moisten it with water. Then children can carefully sprinkle grass seed evenly over the tops of their sponges. Next, have them place their sponges in saucers with a small amount of water. Children can put their saucers in a sunny spot and add water when the sponges begin to dry out. In a few days, they'll see brilliant green grass growing from their sponges!

Indoor Gardening

You will need

herbal plants, such as basil,
* oregano, rosemary, thyme, or*
* parsley*
pebbles
potting soil
small dishes
shoes, worn out or too small
water

Herbal Shoes

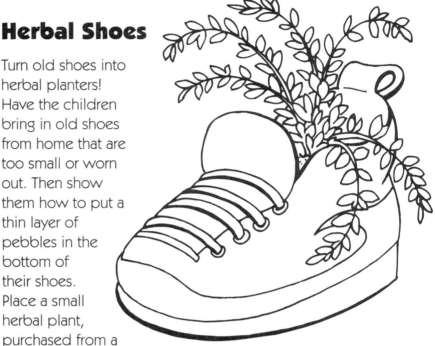

Turn old shoes into herbal planters! Have the children bring in old shoes from home that are too small or worn out. Then show them how to put a thin layer of pebbles in the bottom of their shoes. Place a small herbal plant, purchased from a garden center, drug store, or grocery store, inside each shoe. Help the children pack the plants tightly in the shoes with potting soil. Make sure their Herbal Shoes have appropriate light and water. You may want to keep the plants on small dishes to catch excess moisture. Keep them in a sunny window or invite children to share them with their families.

Painted Pots

This project gives children an opportunity to paint on something besides paper. Give each child a small terra-cotta pot and place the other materials on a table. Encourage children to paint interesting designs on their pots with acrylic paint. After the paint dries, help the children plant flowers, herbs, or plants in their pots, filling in with potting soil. Children can make plant markers on square sheets of paper by drawing pictures of their plants and writing (or dictating) the plant names under their drawings. On the other side, they can write their names and the date so that each child knows which plant is his or her own. Show children how to glue the plant markers onto craft sticks and place them in the pots.

You will need

acrylic paint
craft sticks or recycled frozen
* fruit bar sticks*
flower, herb, or green plant
glue or paste
markers
paper
paintbrushes
potting soil
rounded scissors
small terra-cotta pot
water

Indoor Gardening

Terrific Terrariums

Terrariums make gardening easy! Find clear wide-mouth plastic or glass jars with lids. Give each child a jar and show children how to place a thin layer of pebbles in the bottom. Then have children fill their containers ¼ full with potting soil. Succulents are hearty plants and are usually the ticket to a successful terrarium. One 8-inch succulent gives enough cuttings for several terrariums. Give each child three or four 2-inch cuttings to plant in his or her jar. Help children plant the cuttings root first in the potting soil. After planting, they can lightly sprinkle water over their plants and then screw on the lids. Remind children that succulents need very little water and over-watering is more harmful than under-watering. If their jars are tightly sealed, children may not have to water their gardens. Otherwise, sprinkling them with water every two weeks is usually ample.

Veggie Tops

Turn bare vegetable tops into leafy plants! Cut off the top quarter of unpeeled beets, carrots, sweet potatoes, or white turnips. Give each child a veggie top and invite children to place the tops of their vegetables in shallow bowls of pebbles and water. Water alone will suffice if you don't have pebbles. Place the bowls in a sunny area, adding water when necessary, and within a few days, leafy veggie tops will appear!

You will need

pebbles
plastic or glass jars with lids
potting soil
succulent plant

You will need

beets, carrots, or white turnips
knife (for adult use only)
pebbles
shallow bowls
water

Outdoor Gardening

Planting a garden with the children is a long-term commitment. Not only will you be planting seeds or plants together, but you will also be assisting the growth process of the plants. Children will experience the importance of working together as a team and paying attention to details as they cultivate their garden. They will learn how to plan a project, follow through, and, finally, reap the benefits of their gardening efforts.

Preparing the Soil

Decide with the children where their garden will best flourish. Stake out a vacant area that has the proper sun exposure. Or consider using a window box as your garden. Explain to the children that in order for the garden to grow well, they need to prepare the soil. Have them begin their adventure by removing large rocks and other debris from the soil. While they are on their rock hunts, remind children to pull weeds and throw them away. They can put the rocks aside for later use as a border around their garden. After children remove the rocks and weeds, have them add nutrients to the soil and turn the soil with their shovels.

You will need

nutrients (purchased at garden centers)
small shovels
soil

Outdoor Gardening

You will need

green plants, flowers, herbs,
  vegetables, seeds, or
  cuttings
small shovels
water

Planting

Decide with the children whether their garden will be filled with green plants, flowers, herbs, vegetables, or any combination of these. Then decide whether the garden will begin with seeds, cuttings, small plants, or a combination. Show the children how far apart and how deep they should dig the holes, and let the planting begin. Plant seeds as directed on the seed packages. Plant cuttings and small plants with roots down, leaving plenty of room for growth between plants. Remind children to tap down the soil after planting and then water their seeds and plants thoroughly.

Outdoor Gardening

You will need

fertilizer
liquid soap
paper
pencil
rounded scissors
spray bottle
water

Maintaining

Explain to children that for their garden to thrive, they need to provide it with water, keep it free of weeds, and even fertilize the soil. They may have to spray for bugs with a mixture of 1 part liquid soap and 3 parts water, a mixture that works for many pests. It may be necessary for children to trim back some of their plants for optimal growth. With children, chart the growth differences of the plants. Note which grows the fastest, is the tallest, the shortest, and the healthiest. You may also want to create a garden maintenance calendar. Assign children to specific garden tasks on certain days as they watch their garden grow!

You will need

garden shears or scissors

Harvesting

When it's time to harvest the crop, you and the children can decide if you want to put the crops in a vase, a salad, a pan to cook, or a dish to dip. They might even choose to leave them in the garden! If you and the children decide to harvest your garden, demonstrate how to use garden shears or scissors to properly cut the plants. Flowers should be cut near the end of the stem, but vegetables should be cut near the attachment. Then enjoy your harvest!

skills

Children acquire skills on a daily basis through hands-on learning and experience. Learning new skills or improving old ones through games makes the skill-building easy and fun!

Math

Mathematical skills are used on a daily basis. Through play, the activities here reinforce commonly needed math skills—quantity, measuring, patterning, shape identification, number recognition, and sequencing.

Less and More

You will need

small pretzel sticks

Make this activity an educational snack! While sitting at a table, have each child count out 15 pretzels and divide them into two piles—one pile of five and another of 10 pretzels. Then ask children to point to the pile that has less. Next, tell them to remove seven pretzels from their pile of 10 and form a third pile. Ask them to point to the pile with the most, and so on. As snack time comes to a close, invite children to eat one pretzel at a time, asking them to point out which pile has the most or the least as their piles dwindle in size.

Measuring

You will need

ruler
rounded scissors
string or yarn

Help children discover the difference between their own foot size and a twelve-inch foot measurement. Have the children measure and cut a 12-inch or one-foot piece of string or yarn. With their pieces of string, children can look around the room for objects about the same length. After five minutes, form a circle and ask the children to share what they found. Discuss how their feet measure up to their one-foot pieces of string and which of their objects are the same, longer, or shorter than their strings.

Math

You will need

paper
pencil
rounded scissors

Number Hunt

This Number Hunt gives children practice in writing and identifying numbers. Cut paper into small squares. Help children write the numbers 1 through 20 on separate squares. Then hide the numbers and challenge children to a Number Hunt. Add more challenging twists by having each child search for a specific number, write numbers up to 100, or do simple addition and subtraction. Invite them to alternate hiding the numbers and start the game again.

You will need

construction paper
glue or paste
last year's calendar
rounded scissors

Number Sequencing

Old calendars are great for cutting and pasting projects! Show children how to cut out numbers from one to twenty from a calendar. Together or individually, have children glue the numbers in order onto construction paper. Or have them fold their papers in half and glue odd numbers on the left side of the paper and even numbers on the right side.

Math

You will need

colorful cereal with holes
rounded scissors
ruler
string

Pattern Necklace

Threading cereal onto strings provides a fun snack with a learning opportunity! Help children measure and cut 16-inch pieces of string. Then invite each of them to each take a handful of cereal and sort it by color. Show them how to tie their first piece of cereal to the end of the string. Then discuss how they can form a pattern by threading two reds, three blues, one green, two reds, three blues, one green, and so on. Have the children make up their own original patterns. When they finish threading, knot the two ends of each string together and their necklaces are ready for wearing and nibbling!

Shape Extravaganza

You will need

colored construction paper
glue or paste
rounded scissors

Using shapes only, children can make complete pictures. Make cardboard templates of rectangles, circles, triangles, and squares ranging in size from one inch to four inches. Encourage children to use the templates to trace and cut out different shapes from colored construction paper. Then challenge them to make interesting things out of the shapes. A child can make a car, for example, with a rectangle and two circles. Add a thinner rectangle at the top end of the rectangle to make a handle and turn the car into a wagon. Children can use the shapes to make animals, buildings, boats, and so on. Have them glue different shapes onto sheets of paper to make their own Shape Extravaganzas!

Music

Most children enjoy music. Some children want to be actively involved and play an instrument. Others receive just as much enjoyment by listening, singing, or dancing to music. Music can create moods. Play soft music to calm children or upbeat music to lift their spirits. Play dance rhythms to invite them to use their energy in creative ways. The simple activities below offer a variety of choices for everyone to be part of the musical world.

Conductor

You will need

real or toy musical instruments

Being a musical conductor may help a child discover new talents or interests and gives him or her a chance to lead others. Give each child a chance to be the conductor when a group is singing or playing instruments. He or she can choose the melody or song and begin the music. If several children want to lead, rotate frequently.

Glass Band

You will need

glasses
metal spoons
water, milk, or juice

Snack time is ideal for creating a Glass Band. Give each child a spoon and a glass with a different amount of liquid in it. When children tap the glasses with their spoons, they'll be surprised at the variety of sounds, depending on the liquid level in the glasses. After they randomly tap, have the children sing a favorite song and tap their glasses in time with the song. As children drink their juice and play their music, have them listen for different tones as the levels of their drinks change.

Music

You will need

1" x 2" x 4" pieces of wood
construction paper
dried rice, beans, or popcorn
    kernels
glue or paste
markers
oatmeal boxes
paper plates
plastic bottles
ribbon
rounded scissors
sandpaper
stapler
tape

Homemade Band

Invite children to create their own band! Provide the materials listed here, as well as other appropriate items, for children to use in making instruments. A child can make a tambourine by filling two paper plates with dried rice or beans and stapling or taping the plates together. An empty oatmeal carton acts as a drum. Show children how to make sand scrapers by gluing sandpaper on two 1" x 2" x 4" pieces of wood. Demonstrate how to turn a plastic bottle into a shaker by filling it with popcorn kernels, rice, or beans and adding tiny pieces of colored paper. Markers and ribbon add decoration to the instruments. Once the instruments are complete, let the music begin!

Music

You will need

toy or real piano or xylophone

Xylophone or Piano Play

Invite children to experiment with pitch while playing the musical scale from low to high on a piano or xylophone. Together with children, sing the scale as you play it, moving your hand up in the air as your voices go up. Then give each child a turn to play the scale, while the others move their hands up and down as the sound goes up or down.

To add variety, play two notes, one at a time. Have the children indicate with their hands whether the second note is higher or lower than the first. Give each child a turn to play two or three notes going up or down the scale. Have the others show the up or down movement with their hands.

Science

Children always want to know why or how something works. They remember an explanation better if they are shown the answer to their question. Provided here are science-based activities to help children understand how flowers drink water, what happens when they break surface tension or use a magnifying glass, what is magnetic, and what sinks or floats.

Color Explosion

With the children, pour enough milk to cover the bottom of a pie tin. Encourage them to take turns using an eyedropper to drop food coloring onto the milk surface. Then give each child a toothpick to dip in liquid soap. Show children how to break the surface tension by touching the tip of their dipped toothpick into the milk. Watch the children's expressions as colors "magically" spread!

Colored Flowers

Colored Flowers are novel creations that are a breeze to make! Invite the children to add a few drops of food coloring to a glass of water, then cut one inch from the stem of a carnation and place it in colored water. Discuss with the children how plants drink water through their stems and ask them to predict what will happen to the color of the carnation. Over time, children will gradually observe the veins of the white carnation change to the color of the water. Explain that the water travels through the veins of the carnation stem into the petals until the carnation becomes the color of the water!

You will need

eyedropper
food coloring
liquid soap
pie tin
toothpicks
whole milk

You will need

food coloring
glass of water
rounded scissors
white carnation

Science

You will need

*construction paper
crayons
flowers, leaves, twigs,
    pinecones, or rocks
magnifying glass
small paper bags*

Magnify Nature Walks

Give each child a small paper bag and take the group on a short nature walk. While walking, encourage the children to look for a squirrel, listen to a bird, or find a bug. Invite them to collect flowers, leaves, small branches, pinecones, or rocks from the ground and put them in their paper bags. Upon returning, children can examine their treasures under a magnifying glass. First have them talk about the details they see and then have them draw their treasures as they see them under the magnifying glass.

You will need

*magnets
various items to test magnetism,
    such as nails, stainless steel
    spoons, rubber bands,
    pencils, pieces of cloth,
    ceramic mugs, aluminum foil,
    tin cans, safety pins, drinking
    glasses, paper clips, Q-Tips,
    plastic spoons*

Experimenting with Magnets

Have the children gather a collection of materials, such as those listed at the left. Give the children the opportunity to try to pick up each item with a magnet. Then children can sort the items into two piles—one pile of items that the magnet attracts and another pile that the magnet won't attract. Discuss what is different about the two piles and why the magnet picks up from one group and not the other. Challenge children to take magnets around the room to investigate what other items will and will not attract. Be sure to avoid magnetic contact with personal computers, disks, CD's, and any software, as it will severely damage the equipment.

Science

You will need

bowl or tub

*various small items, such as
    coins, pencils, plastic toys,
    pebbles, small balls,
    toothpicks*

water

Sink or Float

Help the children fill a tub or large mixing bowl with water. Then send the children on a hunt to find small items that can get wet, such as coins, pencils, plastic toys, plastic foam, pebbles, balls, and so on. After the children find their items, have them predict which ones will sink or float by sorting them into two piles. Have each child then drop an item into the bowl. Discuss why some items sink and others float.

You will need

sidewalk chalk

sunshine

Traveling Shadows

This activity teaches children about Earth's rotation and promotes teamwork with an artistic result. Take the children outside on a sunny day and divide them into groups of two. While one child strikes a pose, creating a shadow, the other child traces his or her shadow with sidewalk chalk on the cement or asphalt. Be sure to mark the place where each child is standing as he or she poses. Then have pairs reverse positions. Make sure both the artist's and the model's names are written next to each figure. Discuss what makes shadows appear or move, and talk about why there are no shadows on cloudy days. Have the children return to the same spots two hours later, with each child resuming his or her original pose. Have them observe and discuss the changes in the shadow position as the Earth rotated.

The Senses

Discuss with the children the importance of our senses and how we use them on a daily basis. Ask children in what ways they use each of their senses—hearing, sight, smell, taste, or touch. Also, talk about how each of us depend on our senses for protection.

Just Imagine

This fun activity puts children in touch with all of their senses! Invite children to lie on the floor, close their eyes, and imagine they are at the park, zoo, car wash, grocery store, doctor's office, or other familiar place. Then ask them what they hear, see, smell, taste, and touch. Then ask children to imagine how they would experience the same situation with a missing sense. What would a zoo be like without sight? What would they hear, smell, and touch? What wouldn't they be able to hear, see, smell, taste, or touch in these familiar places if they were missing one of these senses?

You will need

items for use as noise makers, such as pot lids, a pencil sharpener, a faucet, a door, a heavy book, paper

What's That Noise?

Children think they know an object by its sound, but how much of their recognition is sight-based? Choose sounds that children are familiar with, such as two pot lids banging together, a pencil sharpener, water dripping from a faucet, a door closing, a book dropping, crumpling paper, and clapping hands. Have the children cover their eyes and guess what sounds you are making. If possible, make sounds that are not as familiar to the children, such as tapping a plastic cassette or CD case, running your finger on the rim of a wet glass, or tapping a glass with a spoon. Children can try to guess what these sounds are. Then have them take turns making different sounds for each other.

The Senses

I Spy

Point out to the children that, though their eyes are open and they are looking around, they don't always notice detail. I Spy helps make children more visually aware of details around them. Select a child to think about one object in the room and give a clue to describe it. Then the child says to the others, "I spy with my little eye something that is . . . ." The clue may describe the object's color, shape, or size. The other children look around the room and try to guess the object. The first child to guess correctly chooses the next object.

Smells Like . . .

Children are quick to notice yucky and yummy smells. This activity gives them the opportunity to discuss many different odors. Place a variety of foods with distinct odors on a tray. Then blindfold children and challenge them to identify each item by smell only.

You will need

blindfolds

various items with a scent, such as onion, lemon, peppermint, pepper, cinnamon, vanilla, or bubble gum

The Senses

You will need

paper bag
various items to touch, such as feather, banana, marble, book, eraser

Hand in the Bag

When playing this game, children will "see" with their hands instead of their eyes. Choose objects of different sizes, textures, and weights to place in a paper bag. Have the children take turns putting their hands in the bag, and by touch alone, guessing what is inside.

Sweets and Sours

Most children have sensitive taste buds. Sweets and Sours gives them the opportunity to sample familiar foods and be the judge of whether they taste bitter, salty, bland, spicy, sour, or sweet. Select a variety of flavors to judge. While playing the tasting game, emphasize that children shouldn't try unfamiliar foods unless they first ask an adult if the food is safe to eat.

You will need

sweet and sour food items, such as unsweetened chocolate, bread, salted pretzels, salsa, lemon, or brown sugar

Story Extenders

Most children have favorite stories and wish they could make them longer. They can by adding story extenders! Have the children continue favorite stories by adding characters, creating new action scenes, writing sequels, or making crafts that relate to their favorite books. In addition to the ideas below, encourage children to use their imaginations to create their own story extenders individually or as a group.

Corduroy

After reading the book *Corduroy* with the children, ask them who has a Teddy bear or favorite stuffed animal. Invite children to share how they got their Teddy bears and what their Teddy bears mean to them. Then invite children to make their own bears, using the dough recipe found on page 18. Help each child roll one large ball of dough for the body, one medium-sized ball for the head, three tiny balls for the eyes and nose, and six small balls for the ears, arms, and legs. Have the children make sure the balls are snugly secured by dipping the balls in water before attaching them and gently rubbing out the seams to make a Teddy bear.

You will need

Corduroy, *by Don Freeman
(Puffin Book, 1993)*
dough recipe (page 18)
*food coloring or tempera
paints*

Story Extenders

You will need

Goodnight Moon by
    Margaret Wise Brown
    (Harper Collins, 1984)
aluminum foil
cardboard
cardstock
glue or paste
light blue, dark blue, white,
    light yellow and dark yellow
    tissue paper
paintbrush
rounded scissors

You will need

Green Eggs and Ham by Dr.
    Seuss (Random House, 1994)
eggs, one per child
food coloring
ham
large wooden spoon
mixing bowl
nonstick pan
oil
paper plates
plastic knives
whisk or fork

Goodnight Moon

After reading the book *Goodnight Moon* with the children, have them create their own nighttime scenes. Help each child measure and cut a 4-inch moon and several 2-inch stars from cardboard, then cover the shapes with aluminum foil. Next, have children cut or rip small pieces of white, light blue, and dark blue tissue paper for the moons. Suggest children arrange and glue the tissue on the moons by slightly overlapping the tissue paper on the foil-covered cutouts. To make the tissues stick on the foil, have the children brush a mixture of two parts glue to one part water over the top of the tissue. White, light yellow, and dark yellow tissue paper are perfect for the stars. To finish their nighttime scenes, the children can glue the moons and stars onto black cardstock.

Green Eggs and Ham

After reading the book *Green Eggs and Ham* with the children, invite them to make real green eggs and ham! Have each child break one egg into a large mixing bowl. Children can take turns beating the eggs with a whisk or fork. Children can add green food coloring to the eggs before scrambling them. Help children chop ham to add to the eggs as they are cooking. If you don't have a stove available, an electric fry pan is perfect. Then enjoy green eggs and ham for breakfast!

Story Extenders

You will need

The Tale of Peter Rabbit *by Beatrix Potter (Puffin, 1992)*

You will need

The Very Hungry Caterpillar *by Eric Carle (Putnam, 1969)*
coffee filters
egg cartons, cotton balls, or pom poms
eyedropper
food coloring
glue or paste
pipe cleaners
stapler
tempera paint

The Tale of Peter Rabbit

After reading the book *The Tale of Peter Rabbit* with the children, give them an opportunity to role-play the story of Peter Rabbit, his family, and friends. Reread the book. As you read, stop and ask children to pantomime as a group the characters in the story when they appear. For instance, children can hop like bunnies, waddle like ducks, sing like birds, chase like Mr. McGregor, munch veggies like Peter, and stalk like cats.

The Very Hungry Caterpillar

After reading the book *The Very Hungry Caterpillar* with the children, invite them to create their own caterpillar metamorphosis. Give each child a section of an egg carton to paint as a caterpillar. Or you may use pom poms or cottonballs and have children glue them together to make caterpillars. Discuss what caterpillars eat and how long it takes for them to turn into butterflies.

Children can make butterflies by stapling together two cone-shaped coffee filters at the small ends. Next, help them fold pipe cleaners in half and place them on top of the staples to form the bodies. Staple the pipe cleaners in place, and then curl the ends of the pipe cleaners to form the antennae. Help children decorate their butterfly wings by dripping food coloring on the filters with an eyedropper. Children get a thrill out of watching the colors spread as their butterflies take form.

Tactile Activities

Children learn a great deal through touching. When children see something new, often their first reaction is to want to hold it in their hands. But much of the time they are told to look, but not touch. The activities below encourage children to explore through touch.

Cornmeal

You will need

cornmeal
large bowl
tray
utensils, such as funnels,
*   spoons, cups, gelatin molds,*
*   or small cooking utensils*

Playing with cornmeal may seem simple, or silly, but children can play with it almost endlessly! Place cornmeal in a large pan or bowl on a tray to keep the mess contained. Provide funnels, spoons, cups, gelatin molds, and other small cooking utensils to mix, fill, and pour the cornmeal. Discuss with children how the cornmeal feels. Is it cool or warm, soft or hard, smooth or grainy, wet or dry?

Hot and Cold Finger Paint

You will need

bowls
finger-paint paper or
*   construction paper*
various colors of finger paint,
*   including red and blue*

Children can mush and squish and learn as they play with finger paint. Warm a bowl of red finger paint in the microwave. Chill a bowl of blue finger paint in the refrigerator or freezer. Give each child a sheet of paper to experiment with the warm and cool finger paints. Discuss whether the colors or textures change with the different temperatures. Remind children that the color red often indicates hot and the color blue often indicates cold. Have them mix the red and blue together to see what happens. Provide other colors of finger paint for children to create finger-paint masterpieces!

Tactile Activities

You will need

food coloring
plastic or metal containers
water

Ice Sculptures

Ice sculpturing can be a year-round activity! Children can make ice sculptures indoors using trays, or outdoors on cement, grass, sand, or snow. Invite children to fill small containers with water. Help them add food coloring to the water, if they like. Then have them place their containers in the freezer. After the water is frozen, children can work individually or as a group, placing their frozen containers in interesting designs. Once they have created their designs, help them turn the containers over so the ice comes out. Encourage children to rearrange the ice, placing pieces next to each other or on top of each other to create new ice sculptures. Discuss how the water feels before it freezes, then how it feels when it's frozen, and then when it's melting. Talk about what happens when the ice melts and the colors mix.

You will need

salt or sand
tray

Salt or Sand Letters

Some children are kinesthetic learners and learn best through touch. Invite children to write the alphabet, numbers, and their names with their fingers in salt or sand. Place salt or sand on a tray and children can write away. Show them how to gently shake the tray if they want to erase what they wrote. Remind them to keep their hands away from their faces so they don't get salt or sand in their eyes.

Tactile Activities

You will need

food coloring
roasting pan
shaving cream

Shaving Cream Painting

Shaving Cream Painting is an activity that allows children complete freedom of expression because shaving cream is so much fun to touch! Have the children spray shaving cream in a large roasting pan and add a little food coloring. Watch as a Picasso unfolds before your eyes while they make designs or write in the shaving cream.

Your Thoughts

We would love to know what you liked about our book and what you would change. If you have suggestions or additions to our existing activities or ideas for new activities, we want to hear from you. We hope our book is easy to use with rewarding activities that you and the children can hardly wait to do!

So, please, let us hear from you.

Joan Prestine and Debbie Kachidurian
c/o Fearon Teacher Aids
23740 Hawthorne Blvd.
Torrance, California 90505